Yours, Creature

Yours, Creature

Jessica Cuello

JLP

JACKLEG PRESS

JackLeg Press
www.jacklegpress.org

ISBN: 978-1737513438

Library of Congress Control Number: 2022936402

Cover design by Jennifer Harris.
Interior art by Kristine Snodgrass, Asemic work.
Cover art: Madonna (ca. 1895–1896) by Edvard Munch. Original
from The Art Institute of Chicago.

Contents

Absence always could subsume me

He filled my center with forget-me-seeds

And I, in the kitchen, am a genius of famine

A line from the red
radius of your womb
went dark

Mary Godwin Shelley was born to writers Mary
Wollstonecraft and William Godwin. The night of her birth
one of Caroline Herschel's comets went through the sky.

Dear Mother,

I wanted to crawl back into the black interior

of you, womb scratched by an animal—

but they wouldn't let me. I hung apart

like gallows men, dangling for sweet touch.

A line from the red radius of your womb

went dark. That night the whole of London

raised its eyes to watch the comet pass—

except for us. Instead, my currish cry & snarl,

my cuss, my cut-and-run, my cutting tooth,

made death a customhouse.

Your daughter,
Mary Shelley

Dear Mother,

Father noted each event in his diary—
followed by dashes—

wine diet—

doctor visit—

arrival of the puppies—

Your afterbirth would not come out—
the doctor pulled it away in pieces—

Our last meal together—
    —the scalloped wall
    —the paste of blood

and what did father note down then?
that you were pinioned like a bird
that a tomtit sang outside the window
that I didn't hear the song
because my ears were wrapped in cloth

and to expel the placenta
puppies suckled the milk
your body meant for me—

Your daughter,
Mary Shelley

Dear Mother,

Outside the door while
your father raped your mother
you stood like a little god.

I hold a stone
like it's your hand.

The house is gone that killed you:
red-walled, womb of mauve.
I floated inside until it bled like wood

and took a sideways position:
no upright girl: my arm beat
the rib cage with your own urge.

Your daughter,
Mary Shelley

Raised by a dictum, but not a man

Mary Shelley and her half sister Fanny were raised by Godwin with unusual strictness. When the girls were young, Godwin remarried and moved to Skinner Street in London. His new wife brought a third daughter.

Dear Mother,

I am threatened with a return of my girlish troubles,

my arm covered red with scabs, my hand a floor

at the abattoir. At night the animal cry is the clock strike

hour of sour milk. At noon the swinging pig is ankles tied.

In the three stories of the Skinner house my stepmother
    is not you.

Her latch on me is fixed and I learn to regard myself

with her repulsion, fixed to the mould in her domestic eye.

My skin is a revolt. How can it not cry animal

when she pulls my hair and knocks me down.

With longing for your presence,
Mary Shelley

Dear Mother,

I watch G's fingers on the page
Neck with a faint line
Neck you loved

so I love it too
He is the glaze through
which I see the sun

We call the Goat's Beard in our field
Sweet Meadow,
Go-to-bed-at-noon,

and *Wise Father-Men*
I touch the feathered heads
to feel the god of it

At Chalk Farm we drink the cream
of syllabubs
Sister holds my arm but

I am the apple of his eye
I am the reader of his work
His frown can collapse my spine

His grief for you becomes a pillar
my attention winds onto

Are you mad that I took your _____

G. is mad with his glacial love
and becomes more so despite
my maniacal reading toward love:

A child can kill its mother,
baby wet and monstrous, slipping
with eyes opened: black and white,

the stewed creation
not asking to be born,
but requiring _____

M.

Dear Mother,

Labor, labor, little needfire.
You made a nursedom
for a speck of love.

You wrote a ream of neckverse
to stem your father's voice
raging through the walls.

He hanged your dog.
Mother meant penance
by the fire. Nine silent hours.

A secret is a sliver inside.
For you, love was mania
& compulsion, a nunnish

fever at your friend's
bedside. She died in
childbirth, the baby too.

This is my frantic voice,
the mind's *scratch-scratch*
that sits fireside with you.

I kiss your imagined hand,
Mary Shelley

Dear Scottish time,

Father sent me away—or was it stepmother?
To be sent is different from being left.

To be left is to remain in the walls
that repel you. Memory rooms

have no equilibrium. They never match
and Mine so full of him. His turn, his back.

The tilt of the chairs and the cup overflowing.
In that living room, memory is the squinty eye,

a wisp of dress, my father pressing him for a loan.
My Resistance made him large.

In the Scottish time I learned
what it is to be forgotten, to be a dropped

cloth, a middle name,
at arm's length—

&—
Mary Shelley

Dear Mother,

The cadaverous silence of Godwin's children is quite
catacomb-ish
     —*Coleridge*

Silence was my pride, my object stillness,
the quiet-prize   My brain

was a carnation on a stem
made my god-of-a-father look at me:

quiet petals and silver pages
I meant to read until I was his perfect

daughter, but P. put one hand beneath
my smock and all the untouched years

responded   Godwin had nothing
to hold me with   I didn't know

he'd snap me like a stem and toss me
on a pile of exile   He was my god,

first partner, the sun to my green tissue
He sent me letters with formal closings

as though I was still plicate in my room
leaf-ribs pointed toward him,

plumule hidden from all but him
Mother: you didn't raise me

Mary Shelley

Dear Mother,

Scratch beneath the surface of a man
and there's no help. P. disappears

when babies die. There are so many
tasks. Father hated me for being sad.

I pursued ideas like a horse, a dog,
always behind, raised by a dictum,

but not a man. I was a tent-stitch
on the pocket of his mind, a grafted

cut in his bark of book. I cried
in the open (less girl than gnome)

when the bell at the cow's neck
rang *tan-tan-tan* and I took

my first affection
from her wet, black eye.

Yours, as ever, & unmothered,
Mary

Dear London 1814,

Once upon a time
2 half sisters and a stepsister loved the same boy

The boy had his own wife

He left her alone with their child to visit the three sisters

The wife was pregnant

The boy was a poet and grandson of a baronet
His name was Percy Bysshe Shelley

No one lived happily ever after,
Mary Shelley

I dangle from his word.
My life hangs on the
beam of his eye.

Percy Shelley visited the Godwin household as an admirer of Godwin's radical ideas. Godwin wanted money from Shelley.

Percy's wife Harriet was pregnant with her second child when Percy and Mary fell in love.
Percy and Mary met secretly by her mother's grave.
Mary's stepsister Jane acted as their go-between.

Dear Mother,

P. was a little flame with a pale chest
A white shirt open

He sat his sisters hand-in-hand
to electrify them

P. set his house on fire
He was new-light, my laudanum

No was a needle with me
a dull gleam in the old-light

Yes was a light-tower
that seeped through the door
of my lairy room

It grew out of ground
grew risk like millions
like flickers of stars
like pins, black seeds

He was my shiver, blood on the outside

His light-handed rules,
his heavy-handed love

rewrote you, Mother,
and your grave

Yours, trying to explain,
Mary

Dear Mother,

P sleeps before me.
Breathes before me.
I am a tiptoe-face
staring down at his neck.

In fact I was inside a glow
of Godwin and Wollstonecraft.
In fact we were inside a grotto
of our own bodies, coeternal.
Walls of heart cherry, soffits
of flesh. My gaze shone from
the ark of my brain, skin
a coffer of treasures.
I unlatched myself inside
his bed and kept his hundred
gazes in my mind   *for ever*.

Yours at 16 years,
Mary Shelley

Dear Mother,

I left father a farewell note.
He was my former god
and deserved at least a word

before the soft-skinned god
swooped in. I thought I'd die
in that boat. P. took one of his

love poems, crossed out
Harriet and put my name.
Stepsister watched the storm

while I got sick. She played
the faithful & I fell to earth
like the bird who banged

against our window frame.
Poor bird that couldn't
see form. I kneeled

in the wet boat against
the altar of P.'s knees,
swallowed vomit & fear

to place my head there.
The forms of stepsister
beside him in the boat

and his wife at home
meant this god was like
the other gods: thin love

and absent eye
and never enough
god to go around.

Yours affectionately, & seasick,
Mary Shelley

Dear Mother,

I did not write to you so long
because you were angry in my dream.

I crossed the sea with the sick
below. The inner ear

made a separate sea. All three
of us read your book: That's how

I learn your voice and tie it to me.
Jane does too—I share my dead

with her though I am loathe to.
I wonder will this birth bring

dirty doctor hands
as I brought them to you.

Then what trail for her little feet?
Lamb hooves, rough pads. What crumbs?

We tried to find your France
but we met dead fields and hunger.

The backward-looking need no enemies
and every world is provincial once you're in it.

Your pregnant daughter,
Mary Shelley

Dear Mother,

He and I had a bed of brine
where I was salted twice.

In France, P. told me to bathe
in the river but I refused.

Jane said I was too modest.
In a dream I lifted off my dress:

heavy starch and sweat. The salt
of me smelled like old wounds.

I began with you. Your salt.
I lied to P. and said his work was hard

but hard was not a word I used.
I would have sat with knotted songs

in deserts, glacial heights—taken
slow steps. I would not, however,

swim naked off a French road.
Do not ask this_____

Not a salt-wife, no wife at all,
I wanted a salt-meadow to lie in.

Wanted to taste what Jane could not
and what my price had been.

Yours, ever following,
Mary Shelley

(I am awake
I see him now

What better boy than this?)

Dear Mother,

I dangle from his word.
My life hangs on the beam of his eye.

Before father took you in. Did you ever hang?
I think you did not. I think you pure as granite.

Remember the gallows on Mercantile Street.
I am too pulsed and alive to swing. But the crow

has a beak of mockery. The silver eye
insists, repeats. Father taught me that space

began with my fingertip on your letters:

MARY WOLLSTONECRAFT

Your daughter,
Mary

Absence always
could subsume me

Mary Shelley and Percy Shelley were unmarried when she had her first child. Her father refused to see her.

Dear Rejection 1815,

In threes they came: the mother, the father,
the holy lover. One by one they cut me loose:
the first went underground without me.

The second couldn't bear to touch me:
I was monstrous, toddling from bed
with open mouth, a devil girl with spindly

neck. The third was a boy who touched
my thigh to prove that I was nectar-made,
my girlhood gone. He fled whenever I felt

too much. Who can love a second time.
His face was the only male face.
Absence always could subsume me,

powered as it was by the first rejection:
God's holy three of *No No Never.*

Yours, as I have always been,
Mary Shelley

Dear Mother,

Until I have a father
P. can be my father:

Half a father, door-turned
father, father of the residence,

father broke and broken,
father borrowing from

the child, father drubbing,
father pages, father lies.

After the baby died
P. befriended my stepsister.

He made a come-and-go,
an avoidance of my grief bucket,

turned his back on
the careless coma doctor.

He was *A man of many parts*,
made from the legs of me

the chest of her, dissected red
& covered with a poultice.

I'm sewn from gut to brain
with scraps of men.

Ta fille,
Mary

Dear Fanny Blood 1783,

In the household of Blood,
the men like shadows,

she pictured you alone together
her agitation like a thread

knotted on the finger with the tip,
wetted by her tongue

> *A friendship so fervent it was the ruling passion*
> *of her mind*

You with needle, with pencil
turning it to money

Her eyes touched you
even when they turned away

Acicular
bent to a future

> When love is thin every kindness is deep and keen

No one eye could funnel it
She made you larger than you were

and when she leapt from loneliness
she landed in the same room

Tell me what you know,
M.S.

Dear Mother,

My stepsister has changed her name:
Claire clear as light. My omen

is the empty nest with little fluff
of dandelion and thread.

Claire has taken your birthday
for her own. Here's what

I wouldn't tell anyone else:
I want this baby to make him love

the way he did.
Pregnancy has snagged me up,

changed my space. Like his wife
I am isolated with my womb.

Did you know G. would turn
on me when I broke the rules?

We only guess at what you'd do—
would you turn too?

At your stone, tiny daisies
fill the earth with grey-like letters

and weave no spell.
I retreat to books when no one loves.

Yours, as ever,
Mary

Dear January 1784,

She kidnapped her own sister, Eliza,
from a terror that made a whimper

Sister lip sputtered a child cry
hound cry   fox bark   seagull shriek
no sense words   no sense shapes

shoulder shadow on the blank wall
hood   cloak   barrel   nothing there

My mother called it *the other evil*
all women know   Don't name it

Eliza lost custody of her infant daughter
and the baby died shortly after

Yours in 1820,
M.S.
(daughter of M. Wollstonecraft)

Dear 1786,

She said my mother *freed her*.

My mother wrote a book.
Mary, Mary, that rigid story.

Mary had never had any particular attachment   Mary chose
Lisbon rather than France   Mary followed them   Mary was
struck with awe   Mary started   Mary's precautions
Mary had not said much   Mary was obliged   Mary shrunk
back   Mary rose early   Mary endeavored   Mary was
petrified   What a sight for Mary!   Mary kept up some little
formality   And Mary waited

My mother as governess, as companion, as servant.
The hysteric, the frock, the wan complexion.
The desperate for money.
She shook in church. She had two charges.

When the sisters were sick, it was my mother who
nursed them. I met one of these charges later.
Tell me of her, I said.

Never a Governess,
M.S. 1820

Dear North 1795,

She pursued his ship like it was him
like his capital was scraps of skin   like
the cargo was silver love   Laudanum
deadened her   Norway numbed her
The Baltic Sea passed rag after rag
of waves   She stared through it
before she pulled it inside her before
she took it to her lungs   Before she
smothered the pips of need she tracked
his ship   secured the silver cargo
crossed   Norway   Sweden   Denmark
and the whole time she had her baby with her

Yours,
M.S. London 1820

Dear Sweden 1795,

Heart's Ease grew over the rocks:

viola tricolor   wild pansy   heart's delight

johnny-jump-up-and-kiss-me

The pansies grew solitary, lateral.

three faces in a hood   love in idleness

The song they wouldn't play
for dead Juliet was *Heart's Ease.*
It was not the time to play

and I had a father who would relent—
or so I thought. I kept a valve
in my heart trained in his direction,

and before my mother knew him
she wrote that she was *a particle broken
from the grand mass of mankind.*

Faint purple blossoms: common, not needed.
Name a thing a hundred ways

and will it surface? I am underfoot
and scattered, waiting like she
waited. I have not a single memory
of warmth.

And none of her.

Yours,
M. Shelley
(daughter of M. Wollstonecraft)

Dear Mother,

You wrote that you could not avoid the "I"

A person has a right to tell
and I could tell a tale by night

I wrote beside the tossed grey water
and where the dark red rags were soaked

I told by yeast and flour,
made a man, made a monster,
put it on the Chamonix

I told a tale by ice and organ,
made a parcel of desire

After the mountain & dead baby,
P. offered up his friend to love

I tried to conjure some desire
for him

A person has a right to tell
a right to "I"

You wrote this when Imlay left you
(Before you met my father)

But I have met my only love
and I am done with "I"

Your daughter, as ever,
Mary

Dear Sweden, 1795,

She wrote that *an enlarged mind is no use*
and muttered over her dead friend.

She could not mutter over me, unborn:
a fire not yet in her eye. She still gazed

toward the bridge's ledge.
She didn't know I would do it for her:

Be her little murderer. My own afterbirths
came out like floors of flesh, pink animals

the child and I kneaded together. Hers
stayed inside the first room of death.

They put me in a stranger's arms.
But back when they pulled her from

the river where she tried to drown, the room
I would occupy in her was warm.

Yours, in London 1820,
M.S.
(daughter of M. Wollstonecraft)

Dear Mother,

I had a dream
that my little baby came to life again.

What is it to make a life
that dies—like god
it cannot stand
to stay.

Cabbage leaves are soft
like cloth and smell of tea.
I wore them on my breasts
like medicine. The earthy
taste of tea made me hate
my flesh—I didn't know
if I was made of
anything else.
Her thirteen days
were the only time
and they had no measure.
Clouds swirled like bands
of twisted cloth.
I'm sorry to burden you.

As a child, I was spooked
by the empty hall
when father moved us in.
At first he loved me

like I was you

and in the dream *we rubbed it by the fire*
and it lived.

Yours, as ever,
Mary

He filled my center
with forget-me-seeds

I never saw a more interesting creature: his eyes have generally an expression of wildness, and even madness....

Mary's first child died.

In the summer of 1816, Mary Shelley, Percy, her stepsister Jane, and Byron gathered at a villa in the mountains of Switzerland. Here she began *Frankenstein*.

Dear Mother,

I was aware of you *The Year Without a Summer*.
The sunlight reddened.

My hands, too, were *weather backward*.
People looted the warehouses of grain.

It rained red. But we remained corded,
issued from the other. It rained

one hundred days. The river came
to new marks. The world matched

our minds and I invented a doctor
who cobbled together a man.

I who copy you,
Mary

Dear Hotel Guests,

We are in the ether of this baby world

When a food particle clings to a dish
When the baby gums

Where did the little infant go
and what dirt

How will her 13 days go in the ground
and how will she appear in my Italian sleep
the hotel lobby with its eyes

In the hotel registry her father wrote: *L'Enfer*

In the water he wrote no wish
At night we begged in our sleep

Yours (ostracized),
Mary Shelley

Dear Creature,

The sea of ice
was my favorite distraction.

We kept a squirrel
inside a box who bit me.

P. carried him for awhile
the way he carried kindness,

useless & external,
like a man. At night

when we read "Christabel"
P. thought my nipples

were eyes. He ran away—
afraid. I suppose each hole

of my body is an eye.
Especially my mouth—

repulsed by the heat
of its need.

Your monstrous creator,
M.S.

Dear Creature,

After everyone forgot the summer without a summer
I still had the ice indelible

and your parceled face
shifting in visible heat.

I was making sentences for dear life.
And also money. I would know

its particular insecurity
my whole life.

P. was part of making.
But he would not

abandon Claire
when Byron took her child.

I could have left her
behind. I was both

cruelty and lair,
nursemaid and envy.

I could sketch out life
or snuff its current.

54

She had a *named* child.

Your monstrous maker,
M.S.

(Do you know P. ran from our infant who was born too early)

Dear Creature,

Father won't see me either.

I grow used to the side of a door.

Do you know I can feel space extend

beyond me? On ship, the capped

waves made emptiness larger.

Is that why I was seasick?

Jane never was. She and P.

talked on deck. I knew *Below*

as familiarly as the wolf knows

the dark beyond the fire.

I put you there, Creature,

outside the cottage & the woods,

as Jupiter has rings of gas

so none may enter.

Your creator,
Mary Shelley

Dear Creature,

Sister against half sister
Sister against stepsister
The wedge was P.

All three of us jostled
to be in his line of sight
but he had only two eyes

and they saw as one—
monofocused
on a single girl

Half sister took herself out
Stepsister sought eyes
from other men

Deficit as old as food
as old as fire
shining from within

the cottage
Creature, how female
I made you

peering at the family
& gathering their wood—
But they don't want you

Your loving servant,
M.S.

Dear Mother,

P. and I did not play hide and seek.
He left
and I played Seek Seek.

How much of the ice palace will I repeat.
He told me to decide between
Italy and the sea.

I said, *Get your hair cut in London.*

When I was 15
Prima Facie was my due.
Face of mother,
father's face.
Prie-Dieu
was my praying desk.
Preterhuman was a word he made.
We made a man.
I made five lives
and two were lives.
We roped with words
what could not rope.
I tore back

what could not tear—
my pink paper skin
and I made him
a face to learn his face.
My face was his
and it left
enough imprint—
but not enough

Yours in infatuation,
Mary

Dear Creature,

You alone reconcile me to myself
he wrote   and that was what I'd done:

called out his genius from the hall
gave the gift of routine: mealtimes

with meals, a morning to read,
a walk to the oak

He filled a bowl with bread and sugar
He filled my center with forget-me-seeds

In the margins I wrote this fear:
hours with *her*

I had no formal lessons
Years ago Mr. Coleridge kneeled

at our level
to tell the tale of the mariner

Serpent monsters swarmed the floor
and there has always been a man

like a tower light—
and me the swarm

Your faithful creator,
M.S.

Dear Creature,

P. and I read each other's writings
& I am relieved a little of desire.

The child said *Some beings don't live long,*
pointing to the dragonfly.

In my womb the child moved beneath the skin
and lifted the surface in the shape of an arm.

I thought how the other children's arms
were tucked in and never seen.

An arm against—a sack of blue.
Once the hardness of my mind

dropped to the womb.
Creature, you opened

each brain window,
a god that jumped from

ear to ear. Sometimes I listened
for you when I touched P.

You came with his voice.
His hand could draw you.

Your creator,
M.S.

Dear Creature,

I alternate between book and milk.
Pure air and burning sun

We took in a girl called Polly Rose.
She kept my flowered plate.

It's nine months to make a life.
Then you feed and rock their little

forms. You worry them into morning,
then worry them into night.

At Bishop's Gate they carried out
the coffers and the chairs. Money

is an extra skin that keeps some safe.
I tell my boy to stay away

from damaged people. Polly's feet
pass our bedroom door.

She is the neighbor's girl
they couldn't feed. P. brought her

home. He gave away his shoes.
Every woman is damage

& witness, strung invisibly
from baby to man.

Your creator,
M.S.

Dear Mother,

In the grass, the red-self, cardinal,
is nerves.

We are in Albion and I wish Claire
away again.

She left for 9 months and came
back empty.

At night it's hot. My son turns, I hear
him dream.

I hear the linens move with his hot
little limbs.

P. does not attend.
When women return with empty arms

does a line end.
God's line. I stepped in God's tent

when P. first went inside me—
we were at your grave.

Do you know that after his death
I'd keep the muscle

of his heart inside a drawer—
The red-self, dust.

I am without pity for
her woman-pain because—

I am Your callous girl,
Mary

Dear Mother,

I saw the red-brown body of an animal
on the edge of a field. Hesitant.
I read that you stepped into a gutter of blood.

When you reacted a man said, *No.*
Hide that you are appalled
or they'll arrest you.

You were close to the guillotine
and I dreamed that I was like you.
I became an enemy easily, without

trying, with a gasp and a foot.
We both had unwanted limbs.
Together we were an exile of Mary,

never a gaol of likes & yesses.
But Fanny—one half of you—
Fanny lived her years in hideland.

Fanny was a neck of obeisance.
And I let her:
tiny hop, plain flicker of red.

She spent half her time
saying *thank you* & *I'm sorry*
before the quiet suicide.

Your living daughter,
Mary Shelley

Dear _____,

I heard from G. when my half sister died.
Go not to Swansea, disturb not the silent dead.

If a girl is tired of herself, isn't it her right
to leave this world. All this time G. lived

like I was dead. He broke months of silence to write.
There is no crawling back to the beginning,

no rewriting of the child. The tics you get
are yours to get. My sister was folded in—

a passive missive. I was bite. I remember
her room in Swansea where I never went

and I remember the chambermaid who kept
Fanny's wishes and left her alone. Except, *listen*:

she was left alone from start to finish.
We shared one mother who could not be shared.

The living daughter,
Mary Shelley

And I, in the kitchen, am
a genius of famine.

In Italy Mary's second child died, then her third child.
Byron said bury the daughter on the shore.

A miscarriage nearly killed Mary.

Percy drowned in a boating accident.
Mary was 26.

Dear Mother,

You knew what couldn't fit inside
your hut of heart:
a soldier's tent of grief and the living girl.

Alegra dies inside a convent at age 7.
We don't tell Claire.
Nights later P. can't sleep.

He sees Alegra walking on the waves
though she was Byron's child, not his.
For his own dead children,

he doesn't dream. They are buried
under Arctic weight.
We are both inside a den of grief,

but just five years before I sat
at father's table, tuned to
the sharpness of my stepmother,

sipping from a childhood cup
of blue, and my chest cabinet
that held a single shelf for you.

Yours,
Mary Shelley

Dear Creation,

The porcelain basin
has dread in it.

Its film of dust throbbed
in my left temple.
The left eye began its twitch poem.

We pack up and move again.
Gather everything on a cart.
P. does not gather things.
Someone does it for him.
He does not even know
that gathering happens.

He gathered me in the first hotel room
when we got rid of Claire.

He made me shiver over and over.
Seen.
My legs were threads of nerve
and blood. I floated up.

I remember no basin in that room.
I place a hard, white basin
in there now. I give it a grim sketch

of daisies. In the beginning
of basins I started my life laboratory:
either the mother-death
or the washing of a child
in a basin of red.

Yours,
M.S.

Dear Mother,

We rent a house in Italy.
Black currants stain our
fingerprints. We write in red —
mother and child. My skin
remembers P.'s glyptic touch:

the sex we had beside your grave.
When I was 15 his words were
earnest like a slingshot.

We gospelized you.

I prepare fermented fish.
The tiny blade lifts the bones
like threads. P. is a genius of wander
and invention. Not one domestic task
takes his attention.

And I, in the kitchen, am a *genius of famine*.

Your loving daughter,
Mary Shelley

Dear Creature,

Because of what I did
Society never let me in.

Dim-witted towns don't
see you, but I still remember
the tactile coolness of earth
beside my mother's grave
and P.'s dry hand,
first on my face,
then pressed to the second
heartbeat between my legs.

I spent the rest of my life
scrambling to get back
alone with him —

Because of what I did,
because of this
no prayers went up:

a wall attached to my growth
and tree-knot child, curled black worm
glistening on the shore. Foam child.

Wave father—he couldn't even swim.

Your loving creator,
M.S.

Dear Italy,

Buried at The Lido
with no marker
the way he said

my girl under the sand

The boy still living

but she was in the sand

Buried at The Lido
her fever gone
convulsions ended

Did I travel with her
Did I say *yes* for *no*

yes for him
not *no* for her

Buried at The Lido
with no marker
the way he said

Everything I killed for love
crawl & scramble
pit & labor

is buried at The Lido

with no marker
the way he said

Yours, briefly,
Mary Shelley

Dear Mother,

His wife was Harriet

I think of her and little Ianthe

Thomas Peacock asked her what I did

What I did to seduce P.
What I did to steal him

She said: *Nothing*

but that her name was Mary,
and not only Mary, but Mary Wollstonecraft

There is *nothing* in my arms
another *nothing*
added to the *nothing* first
the *nothing* second

How do you think of punishment?
Girls make their own

Did you guess your name
would get me love
and blame?

Did you guess I'd build a torture table
in my head?

Did you guess that we would lose
and lose again
what skin we formed
and face we made?

Yours,
Mary Shelley

Dear Mother,

I am always looking at the horizon
though I hate the sea.

I made a list of babies:
not all mine.

I tried to make a man
encompass three: William, Clara, Percy.

There was one that tried to kill me:
nameless.

I wanted it to be my murderer:
little vengeance of your death:

little redress of adultery.
P. plunged me to the waist in ice

and I froze at last.
He saved my life.

When the first child died
I wrote to G.

He wrote back:
What is it you want that you have not?

You are among the worst...
with all this grieving *for a child.*

P. built a boat. He wanted a sea-change,
a churning.

He wanted to be thrown about.
P. can't bear me downward.

He wants me propped up
as I was—

Your grieving daughter,
Mary

Dear Mother,

I sailed with P. before he sailed.
What do you make of birth?
How do you sound out love?
The brittle crushing and the shame.

I will be the cliche I am:
longing for a man
& the stinging of the sea.

After one tiny body
another tiny body.

At twenty-five the wool tunnel of loss
squeezed me dry. I wore pastel colors
so I could dream.

The last corpse had
a white-washed blanket face,
a twist of gray, a luminous
burning on the shore, but I knew,
even when the men didn't,
that the light they called supernatural
was lyme.

My chest cabinet had a little fist
inside. The left arm flapped
with grief. In another life

it was a wing and only P. knew
my full-blown name.

What if it's true that I was
a cold wife like they said?

I didn't go to see him burn.

Trelawny took a jawbone.
Leigh Hunt broke off
another piece of bone.
Pieces of a man to men.
What didn't burn was in his chest.
A tug of tissue, a knot of grief
and still I had to beg
for what was mine:_____

Yours, always left,
M.S.

Notes

A line from the red radius of your womb went dark

Mary Wollstonecraft's placenta would not come out and a doctor was sent for. The doctor pulled it out, but he infected Wollstonecraft who died 10 days later. One of the strange details from the birth is that puppies were brought in to suckle at Wollstonecraft's breasts and draw out her milk.

Raised by a dictum, but not a man

Mary Shelley was raised by her father Godwin. He also adopted Mary Wollstonecraft's daughter Fanny who was conceived from Wollstonecraft's earlier relationship with a businessman named Imlay. Godwin preferred Mary and believed her superior to Fanny, but he raised both girls with unusual strictness and little affection. When the girls were young, Godwin remarried and moved to Skinner Street in London. His new wife had a daughter who was Mary's age. This new wife was hard on Mary.

In *"I am threatened with a return..."* the line is from Mary Shelley's letter to Jane Williams, March 1823, *The Letters of Mary Wollstonecraft Shelley, Vol. I,* ed. Bennett

"In the Scottish Time" refers to a period when Godwin and her stepmother sent Mary away to Scotland at age 15.

The Coleridge quote is taken from Fiona Sampson's *In Search of Mary Shelley.* Pegasus Books Ltd, 2018.

I dangle from his word. My life hangs on the beam of his eye.

Percy Shelley first visited the Godwin household as an admirer of Godwin's radical ideas. Godwin wanted Shelley to loan him money but did not approve of a relationship between Mary and Percy since Percy was already married. In fact, Percy's wife Harriet was pregnant with her second child when Percy and Mary fell in love. Percy and Mary met secretly (by her mother's grave!) and Mary's stepsister Jane acted as a go-between. (Mary's half sister Fanny was kept in the dark.) Mary and Percy ran away together and sailed to France. Jane came too and remained with them for nearly the entirety of their relationship. Both Jane and Fanny were probably in love with Shelley too.
They chose France because Mary's mother had lived there during the revolution, and they idealized it as a place of radical thought and freedom. While they

traveled, they read aloud from Wollstonecraft's travel memoir *Letters Written from a Short Residence in Sweden, Norway, and Denmark.* Mary was pregnant at the time.

In "I dangle from his word..." the line *My life hangs on the beam of his eye* is in MWS's letter to Hogg, January 1815, *The Letters of Mary Wollstonecraft Shelley, Vol. I,* ed. Bennett.

Absence always could subsume me

Mary Shelley and Percy Shelley were unmarried when she had her first child. Due to her unmarried status, her father refused to see her when she and Percy returned to London. Her stepsister still lived with them. After the death of her first child, Percy withdrew and spent a lot of time with Mary's stepsister, Jane. Godwin had written a memoir of Mary's mother that included details of Wollstonecraft's childhood, her intense friendship with Fanny Blood, her affairs, and her suicide attempts. Fanny Blood (her half sister's namesake) is also mentioned in Wollstonecraft's travel memoir.

Mary was never formally educated. Her education began in her father's library and later she imposed on herself an intense schedule of reading and study.

In "Dear Fanny Blood" the line *A friendship so fervent...* is from Godwin's. *Memoirs of the Author of 'The Rights of Woman'*. Penguin.

In "Dear 1786" the middle section is from Wollstonecraft's *Mary*. Penguin.

In Dear January 1784, Dear Sweden, the lines: *the other evil, a particle broken...*, *a person has a right to "I"*, and *"An enlarged mind..."* are all from Wollstonecraft's *Letters written in Sweden, Norway, and Denmark*.

In "I had a dream..." the italicized lines are from Mary Shelley's letter to Hogg after her premature baby dies.

He filled my center with forget-me-seeds

In the summer of 1816, Mary Shelley, Percy, her stepsister Jane, and Byron gathered at a villa in the mountains of Switzerland. It was known as "the summer without a summer" due to a volcanic eruption that filled the atmosphere with ash.

Mary's first baby died 13 days after it was born. Mary spent most of her life with Percy in social exile due to her unmarried status. During the famous summer in Switzerland where she began *Frankenstein*, Percy signed L'Enfer (hell) in the hotel registry.

In "P. and I played hide and seek" the italicized lines were taken from Charlotte Gordon's Biography *Romantic Outlaws*.

Mary and Percy moved many times and were beset with poverty and debt. Mary tried to earn money with her writing.

In "Dear Creature" the line *you alone reconcile me to myself* is taken from *Letters from PBS*.

In "Dear Creature" the line *pure air & burning sun* is a line of Mary Shelley's quoted in Gordon's biography. Percy Shelley often had moments of spontaneous generosity, such as giving away his own shoes. During one period, they let the poor child (Polly Rose) of a neighbor live with their family.

In "In the grass, the red self": it is suspected that Percy also had an affair with Mary's stepsister Claire (she changed her name from Jane). At one point, Claire was sent away for 9 months. There is a record of Percy registering the birth of a child to Mary during a time in which she hadn't given birth.

In "Until I Have a father..." is from a letter quoted in Miranda Seymour's *Mary Shelley* (John Murray Publisher, Ltd., 2000). And "a man of many parts" is Shelley herself quoting from *Prometheus* by Milton.

Mary's half sister Fanny committed suicide in a hotel in Swansea. *Go not to Swansea...* is from a letter from Godwin to Mary Shelley telling her not to pursue the circumstances of her half sister's suicide. The letter is quoted in Gordon. Fanny was Mary Wollstonecraft's child from an earlier relationship, but Godwin raised her. It is suspected that she also was in love with Percy Bysshe Shelley.

The line in the above poem that says "Except, *listen..*" borrows language and syntax from Brigid Pegeen Kelly's "Song."

In "Harriet was his wife's..." the italicized lines from Thomas Peacock's conversation with Harriet (Shelley's wife) are taken from Gordon's biography.

And I, in the kitchen, am a genius of famine.

The lines from Godwin in the poem "I am always looking..." are quoted in Gordon. In this letter, Godwin critiques Mary Shelley for her grief at her child's death. Mary's stepsister Claire had a child with the poet Byron; he took the child from her, and the child died in a convent. In Italy Mary's second child, and then her third child, died.

Byron recommended burying the daughter on the Italian shore (The Lido). While in Italy, Mary also had a miscarriage that nearly killed her.

In "We rent a house..." *genius of famine* is from Shakespeare's *Henry IV*.

Percy drowned in a boating accident when Mary was 26.

In "I sailed with P. before he sailed..." the line 'After one tiny body / Another tiny body..." is a loose homage to Lorine Neideker's poem "Who Was Mary Shelley?"

Acknowledgments

Deep gratitude to the Saltonstall Foundation who let me rent a room for a few days in the winter months. This quiet space is dear to me.

To Annie Finch, who first read this manuscript and helped me discover the order. To Natasha Sajé, who brought the poems closer to lyric. To dear friends Barbara Ungar, Lena Bertone, and Jane Springer, who read early drafts. Special love to Jane, who taught me how to go camping.

To Lucie Brock-Broido who is the teacher I never met.

To Airea D. Matthews for her blurb and generous spirit.

To the entire JackLeg family, especially Simone Muench, Jen Harris, and Suzanne Frischkorn.

Many thanks to the editors of the following publications were these poems first appeared:

American Literary Review: "Dear Mother, [I had a dream]"
American Poetry Journal: "Dear Mother, [I wanted to crawl back into the black]"
Beloit Poetry Journal: "Dear Mother, [Labor, labor]"; "Dear Mother, [Scratch beneath]"

Birdfeast: "Dear Mother, [I sailed with P]"

ellipsis...: "Dear Mother, [I dangle from his word]"

Jet Fuel Review: "Dear Mother, [Until I have a father...]";
"Dear Creature, [I alternate between book and
milk...]"; "Dear Mother, [In the grass, the red-self,
cardinal...]"; "Dear ___, [I heard from G. when my
half sister died...]"; and "Dear Mother, [You knew
what couldn't fit inside...]"

Journal Nine: "Dear Mother, [I Am Threatened...]"

The Literary Review, "Dear Mother, [He and I had a bed of
brine]"

Los Angeles Review: "Dear Creature, [After Everyone]";
"Dear Creature, [The Sea of Ice]"

Mid-American Review: "Dear Mother, [The Year Without
a Summer]"

Mom Egg Review: "Dear Mother, [P. and I did not play
hide and seek]"; "Dear Mother, [We rent a house in
Italy]"; "Dear Mother, [Silence was my pride]"

Plume: "Dear Creature, [Because of what I did]"

Poetry Is Currency: "Dear Mother, [P. was a little flame
with a pale chest]"; "Dear North 1795,"

The Account: "Dear Mother, [Father noted each...]; "Dear
January 1784"

Tinderbox Journal: "Dear Mother, [I did not write to you
so long]"; "Dear Mother, [I watched G's fingers on
the page]"

JACKLEG PRESS

V. Joshua Adams, Scott Shibuya Brown, Brittney Corrigan, Jessica Cuello, Barbara Cully, Alison Cundiff, Suzanne Frischkorn, Victoria Garza, Reginald Gibbons, D.C. Gonzales-Prieto, Neil de la Flor, Joachim Glage, Caroline Goodwin, Kathryn Kruse, Meagan Lehr, Brigitte Lewis, Jean McGarry, D.K. McCutchen, Jenny Magnus, Rita Mookerjee, Mamie Morgan, Karen Rigby, cin salach, Jo Salas, Maureen Seaton, Kristine Snodgrass, Cornelia Maude Spelman, Peter Stenson, Melissa Studdard, Curious Theatre, Gemini Wahhaj, Megan Weiler, David Wesley Williams

jacklegpress.org

Ingram Content Group UK Ltd.
Milton Keynes UK
UKHW010640160523
421832UK00004B/101

9 781737 513438